Really?

Ocean

W9-BSG-789

SCHOLASTIC

New York   Toronto   London   Auckland
Sydney   Mexico City   New Delhi   Hong Kong

Contents

Want to meet some cool ocean scientists? Dive in!

Copyright © 2015 by Scholastic Inc.

All rights reserved. Published by Scholastic Inc., *Publishers since 1920.* SCHOLASTIC and associated logos are trademarks and/or registered trademarks of Scholastic Inc.

No part of this publication may be reproduced, stored in a retrieval system, or transmitted in any form or by any means, electronic, mechanical, photocopying, recording, or otherwise, without written permission of the publisher. For information regarding permission, write to Scholastic Inc., Attention: Permissions Department, 557 Broadway, New York, NY 10012.

ISBN 978-0-545-80650-3

10 9 8 7 6 5 4 3 2 1   15 16 17 18 19

Printed in the U.S.A.   40
First edition, January 2015

Scholastic is constantly working to lessen the environmental impact of our manufacturing processes. To view our industry-leading paper procurement policy, visit www.scholastic.com/paperpolicy.

Team Ocean

Philippe Cousteau Jr., President of EarthEcho International (www.earthecho.org).

Professor Barbara Block, Stanford University. Tuna enthusiast and expert.

Dr. Paul Butler, Bangor University, Wales. Mollusk specialist.

Professor Shin Kubota, Kyoto University, Japan. Immortal jellyfish keeper and expert.

James Maclaine, Fish Curator, Natural History Museum, UK. Looks after more than half a million fish specimens (mostly pickled, stuffed, or dried).

Dr. Jairo Rivera Posada, James Cook University, Australia. Crown-of-thorns starfish expert.

Christian Sardet, Observatoire Océanologique de Villefranche-sur-Mer, France. Creator of the Plankton Chronicle films.

Dr. Tierney Thys, marine biologist, filmmaker, National Geographic Emerging Explorer, and *Mola mola* researcher.

Professor Cindy Lee Van Dover, Duke University. Deep-sea biologist and former pilot of *Alvin*.

One of my earliest memories is swimming in the Mediterranean Sea with my grandfather (the famous ocean explorer Captain Jacques-Yves Cousteau). Growing up watching his films sparked my fascination with the ocean. I love that only 5 percent of the ocean has been explored. I love that the ocean keeps us alive every day! It gives us food and a third of the oxygen we breathe.

ocean

Sadly, our seas are in trouble due to overfishing, pollution, and climate change. We need to fix these problems. In this book, you will meet ocean scientists who are making wonderful discoveries that may help. If we all work together, we can rescue our beautiful oceans. It's never too late.

PHILIPPE COUSTEAU JR.
President of EarthEcho International
www.earthecho.org

Exploring our

People have explored less than 5 percent of Earth's oceans. We have better maps of Mars than of the ocean floor! Yet, every day, thousands of men and women put on their diving suits and risk life and limb to learn about this fantastic habitat. In this book, you'll find out about some of their most incredible (and weird!) discoveries.

No fish? What's going on?

Earth is getting hotter. This pattern is called climate change. It is destroying areas of our ocean and the animals that live in them.

oceans

amazing scientists who explore them!

prove it!

One heroic scientist is Professor Barbara Block. She has been part of a huge mission to tag thousands of sea creatures, such as tuna, sharks, elephant seals, and turtles. The animals have to be caught very carefully, so as not to hurt them, and tagged one by one. Satellites track them and scientists study their movements.

RESULTS

"By tagging predators, we can track where they move, eat, and breed. It has produced some great results! We hope that as we know more, we can protect key areas of the ocean."

the

"I love being an ocean scientist because I get to explore our incredible coral reefs. Each time I dive, there is always something new to see. Reefs are home to so many extraordinary ocean animals. By helping protect them, we are helping protect our own future."

DR. JAIRO RIVERA POSADA

(see page 19 for more about Dr. Rivera Posada)

reef

Life on the

Coral isn't just a pretty rock face. Coral is alive!

Ocean scientists find coral reefs fascinating, because they are teeming with life. But divers have to watch out—reefs can be dangerous!

Look closer!

A polyp is basically a tiny stomach with a tentacled mouth!

Look closer

Coral is a living structure made up of tiny animals called polyps. The polyps sit on the surface of the structure. The rocky part beneath is made up of skeletons of old polyps.

Reefs are home to 25 percent of all marine life.

Coral's deadly enemy

This starfish may look harmless, but this prickly pest can wipe out huge areas of reef. Find out more on pages 18–19.

Climate change and pollution are big threats to coral. A lot of

reef

After a full Moon, coral sometimes shoots **MILLIONS** of little eggs into the sea—like an underwater snowstorm! They will become new polyps.

Survival on the reef

The reef is filled with creatures that have to eat while avoiding being eaten themselves. It's a perilous place!

Coral grows **VERY SLOWLY**—only 0.1 inches to 4 inches per year.

Many animals, like the sea anemone, are extremely venomous.

Octopuses change their skin color for camouflage.

The woolly reef is still growing!

In 2005, a group of people started crocheting a reef out of yarn. The yarn reef now tours the world, helping people become aware of how humans are destroying coral reefs.

coral dies every year. We must save it.

11

Stunning shrimp

Check out the pistol shrimp!   **Underwater photos amazed**

The tiny, 2-inch-long pistol shrimp has a fascinating way of killing its prey: It snaps its massive claw at amazing speeds. A team of scientists watched pistol shrimp closely. This is what they saw:

1 The shrimp waits for an unsuspecting crab to wander past.

2 As the crab approaches, the shrimp releases its claw—SNAP!

3 The claw shuts at an astonishing 62 miles per hour, releasing a tiny bubble.

4 The bubble bursts with an enormous BANG, so loud it could burst your eardrum!

5 The sound stuns the crab. It can't move. It's ready to be gobbled up.

During World War II, submarines hid near colonies of pistol shrimp. The noise of the snapping hid the sound of the submarines' sonar.

prove it!

Don't be tempted to keep a pistol shrimp as a pet! When it snaps its claw, the sound can **shatter** aquarium glass!

So how does this tiny animal's stun gun really work? To find out, a team from Germany and the Netherlands set up a very expensive camera that could take pictures at a rate of 40,000 frames per second. They placed a shrimp on a platform, next to the camera and a microphone. Then they tickled its back with a paintbrush—and SNAP!

The sound of lots of pistol shrimp snapping at the same time is the loudest noise in the ocean!

RESULTS
The hugely high pressure and temperature inside the bubble cause the loud BANG as the bubble bursts. They also produce a flash of light as hot as the surface of the Sun! The prey is completely stunned.

Reef geniuses

The reef animals squid, octopuses, and cuttlefish are called cephalopods. Scientists are studying how amazingly smart they are! They can figure things out, like humans do.

A cephalopod can change its skin when it needs to camouflage itself. Its skin may change colors, textures, or patterns!

Some squid can shoot

Workers at an aquarium in the UK once noticed that their tank of lumpfish had one fewer fish in it each morning. Then they discovered that an octopus was climbing out of its tank every night, crawling over to the lumpfish, gobbling one up, and clambering back to its own tank!

An octopus's arm has a mind of its own.

Scientists watched a disconnected octopus arm crawl away on its own. When the arm found food, it tried to feed its missing body!

And guess what else—octopuses can regrow their arms!

Watch out!

Cephalopods squirt ink when they are angry or scared.

At a **sleepover** at a zoo, SCIENTISTS found out . . .

. . . that **cuttlefish** dream while they **sleep!**

Z Z

Coral crisis

Sometimes it's the silent killers that are the deadliest.

The future of coral is in peril. It has a deadly enemy—the crown-of-thorns starfish. Scientists are waging war on this prickly predator, which eats coral at an amazing rate!

The crown-of-thorns starfish throws up its stomach onto the coral to eat it!

The starfish's prickles can be very

It can be healthy to have a few starfish on a reef. But when their numbers shoot up, they can **wipe out** whole reefs.

prove it!

Dr. Jairo Rivera Posada has studied the starfish problem on the Great Barrier Reef off Australia. His team has found that human-made pollution helps starfish breed much more quickly. "One starfish can produce up to 60 million eggs, so the number of starfish can quickly get out of control!" he says.

In the 1990s, divers removed 100,000 starfish from the Red Sea coral reef by hand, saving hundreds of acres of reef.

Save the Red Sea!

RESULTS

The team has come up with a way of killing the starfish that is safe for other creatures. Divers managed to remove 27,000 starfish from the Great Barrier Reef in eight days. But it's going to be a long fight to get rid of this prickly pest!

painful to humans. This makes it hard to grab the starfish and pull it off!

BEAUTY OR BEAST?

These reef beauties can turn into beasts if they're hungry!

Plant or animal?

It has recently been discovered that these beautiful but venomous anemones are half plant, half animal! Which part is which?!

Goo-goo . . . GULP!

A sand tiger shark never has more than one baby at a time—because that baby eats all of its brothers and sisters before they're born!

The pinecone fish has natural headlights in its jaw that help it find prey at night!

Arghh!

STING STEALER

The nudibranch eats venomous jellyfish, saving the stinging cells in a pouch. Then it uses the stingers to defend itself.

Quick killer

This cone snail doesn't need to chase its food. Its venomous spike kills so quickly that prey dies instantly and falls right in front of it!

SUCKER!

The frogfish balloons its mouth to 12 times its original size, then sucks in its prey like a vacuum cleaner does!

SMASH AND GRAB

The mantis shrimp packs a big punch with its claws, smashing its prey to death.

ocean

"Whenever I dip my head underwater, I know I'm going to see something that makes me stop in my tracks and ask, *why?* The water transports me into a world where I can somersault, swim, and sidle right up to my study subjects. What more could a biologist ask for?"

DR. TIERNEY THYS

(see pages 42–43 for more about Dr. Thys)

Life in the

The open ocean is home to some of the biggest, brainiest,

There are **16,700** known species of fish.

THINK BIG!

Megaschool

Scientists have found that herring form giant schools that cover dozens of square miles.

Megafish

The biggest animals in the world live in the ocean. This 40-foot whale shark is the largest fish.

There's enough water in the ocean to fill 352,670,000,000,000,000,000

ocean

and most bizarre animals on Earth!

The ocean is so huge that no one knows exactly how much wildlife lives there or what it all looks like. All we know is that it is packed with life. Marine scientists love the open ocean because there is so much yet to discover there.

jellyfish

giant ocean sunfish

There are nearly **250,000** known marine species.

Megajourney

Some animals take LONG journeys across the ocean. Recently, a leatherback turtle was tracked swimming over 12,000 miles just to find its favorite snack—jellyfish!

tuna

teeny-weeny plankton

Minicreatures

The ocean is also filled with billions of microscopic life-forms called plankton.

About **98 percent** of ALL the **water** on Earth is salty and undrinkable.

Plankton

It's difficult to study plankton, because most of it is so tiny. Plankton is made up of any life-form (plant or animal) that is too small to swim against ocean currents. It can gather into huge masses like thick soup, called blooms. If you want to be a plankton expert, grab your microscope!

Hello, big eyes!

Copepods, plankton with shells, can survive in freezing Arctic waters or on boiling vents.

prove it!

IS PLANKTON IMPORTANT?

you decide

Plankton expert and filmmaker Christian Sardet is part of the team leading the Tara Oceans project. Since 2004, the project has sent a scientific yacht to every ocean to collect plankton samples. The latest expedition was to the Arctic Ocean.

Many big sea creatures are plankton when they are tiny larvae (babies)

A teaspoon of seawater can contain over 1 million tiny creatures.

what you might find?

Plankton can be seen from space!

Plant plankton produces oxygen, which we breathe. ➤ When plankton dies, it sinks to the seafloor. Eventually it becomes oil! ➤ It is food for millions of sea creatures, which we eat. No plankton, no fish.

RESULTS The Tara scientists discovered many new species on their 155,000-mile journey all over the world! Plankton is an excellent gauge of the health of the oceans, and studying plankton has shown that climate change is affecting ocean life.

It can be hard to tell what kind of adult a minuscule larva will become!

You are more likely to be knocked out by a falling coconut than eaten by a shark. HOWEVER— if a tiger shark has its eye (and the rest of its senses) on you, you're in big trouble!

Amazing senses

You may think your senses are pretty sharp, but imagine trying to find and catch a speedy fish underwater.

Sharks have more senses than humans do.

Humans have five main senses. Tiger sharks have the same five senses, plus they can also sense electric currents and water pressure. If you are within 3,000 feet of a tiger shark, WATCH OUT!

A tiger shark can taste and touch prey when it catches it.

150 ft.

It can sense its prey's electric field from 150 feet away.

300 ft.

It can see and smell prey and sense its vibrations from 300 feet away.

It can hear prey from 3,000 feet away!

3,000 ft.

Ouch!

Watch out, dude!

The island of Maui, in Hawaii, is having more tiger shark attacks than it did in previous years. Scientists are now tagging the sharks to see if Maui has become a popular new feeding ground for them. If so—look out, surfers!

Tiger sharks have enemies, too! **Three orcas** (killer whales) were recently filmed working together to take down a huge tiger shark.

A drum, a license plate, and a suit of armor! CAR TIRE Once, even a HORSE!

Tiger sharks eat anything! You won't believe what's been found in their stomachs!

TENNIS BALL

handbag

SHOE

torpedo

HUMAN HAND

tin can

SEAL

Lethal

In the ocean . . . watch out, humans!

Crunch!

Great white sharks attack humans out of curiosity. But since they are 20 feet long and have 300 teeth, their curiosity can be deadly to us!

Great white sharks are responsible for **one-third** of all shark attacks on humans.

The jagged wounds delivered by a moray eel are packed with nasty bacteria that cause a horrible infection. OUCH!

Chomp!

BOX OF DELIGHTS

Each box jellyfish has enough poison to kill 60 people!

ROAR!

One touch from a lionfish spine can cause severe breathing problems.

ENORMOUS leopard seals, which can be 10 feet long, have been known to attack divers and inflatable boats.

FLYING DAGGERS
Night fishermen have been stabbed by needlefish flying out of the water!

Speedy biter

If food is scarce, the saltwater crocodile will attack at alarming speed. It can tear the limbs off a human in seconds.

RISKY SNACK!

In the last ten years, more than 20 people have died from eating puffer fish. But if you just avoid the highly toxic skin and organs, you'll be fine!

The stingray has a venomous barb in its tail. The barb—which can kill—can break off in a victim's body.

STING in the TAIL

OW!

Divers who step on stargazers may get very painful stings.

NEED A LIFT?

AN URCHIN CRAB carries a **spiky,** venomous SEA URCHIN. Now nothing will attack the crab! And the sea urchin gets a free ride. Everyone's happy!

Bluefin tuna

You may have tasted tuna from a can, but you won't see this fish in a home aquarium. It can grow bigger than a horse! Tuna are some of the largest and fastest fish in the open sea. They swim in huge schools and are among the ocean's top predators.

A bluefin tuna:
can weigh up to 2,000 pounds

A horse:
weighs, on average, about 1,100 pounds

Too fast to breathe
A tuna swims too fast to absorb oxygen from the water flowing over its gills. Instead, it swims with its mouth open, taking in oxygenated water. If a tuna stops swimming, it suffocates!

A bluefin tuna can reach **45 mph**. It's one of the fastest fish in the ocean!

An Atlantic bluefin tuna can cross

Tuna **NEVER close their eyes and NEVER stop swimming!**

Scientists think that small pieces of the metal **magnetite** in a tuna's head act like a built-in **compass**, helping the fish navigate.

People have been eating tuna for 5,000 years. But it is only now that we are in danger of fishing them to **extinction**.

A tuna can live up to 40 years!

Hunting in teams

Tuna have been spotted hunting together in large groups, herding mackerel into tight balls and picking them off one by one.

A tuna has sharper vision than any other bong fish.

The strong tail powers it through the water.

The flat torpedo shape helps it skim through water.

Retractable fins make the tuna streamlined.

The immortal

Imagine living forever—that's an impossible idea, right?

When this jellyfish finds life hard or dangerous, it starts all over again! It's a little like if, at age ten, you decided to become a two-year-old. And the jellyfish can keep doing this over and over and over again. Scientists think it could go on forever! That's why we call it the immortal jellyfish.

How does it work?

1 The jellyfish sinks to the ocean floor. It loses its tentacles and becomes a jellylike blob.

2 After several days, it produces an outer shell. It sends out shoots that become polyps.

3 Each polyp produces a new jellyfish, exactly the same as the old one.

The population of this jellyfish is exploding oceanwide. That's not very

jellyfish

Not for the   immortal jellyfish!

prove it!

For 15 years, Japanese professor Shin Kubota has kept the world's only captive population of immortal jellyfish. He feeds and studies them every day and has watched their whole rebirth cycle many times. He has also written and performed pop songs about jellyfish!

This is the only animal we know of that can GO BACK IN TIME!

RESULTS

"Once we determine how the jellyfish rejuvenates itself, we should achieve very great things. My opinion is that we could become immortal ourselves."

However . . .

The jellyfish has to stay alive to keep renewing itself, of course. Some sea creatures find it a very tasty snack!

surprising, since it's IMMORTAL!

The open ocean is alive with sounds—from clicks and pops

The mantis shrimp vibrates its shell. It produces a loud **RUMBLING** sound. The sound of many mantis shrimp rumbling together can be earsplitting!

Wailing whales!

Rumble!

People on the coast of Florida were disturbed by a **LOW THROBBING** sound. It turned out to be the sound of fish called black drums!

The male oyster toadfish **WHISTLES** to attract females. It flicks its muscles against its swim bladder (an organ full of gas) 200 times a second.

ANYBODY OUT THERE?
The blue whale is the
SECOND-LOUDEST animal
on Earth. It can be heard
500 miles away!

A **LOUD SCRAPING** noise on a New Zealand reef was found to be the sound of sea urchins using their mouths to scrape algae off rocks.

PARDON ME!
Herring talk through their bottoms! When they break wind, they make a BUZZING sound.

SQUEAK!

The spiny lobster makes a **SQUEAKY, RASPING** sound with its antennae— just like a violin.

POP!

It has recently been discovered that clown fish use their **CLACKS** and **POPS** to show one another who's boss.

Smart dolphins

They play games, use tools, and even talk to one another!

Dolphins are really smart. Their brains are AMAZING! As far as we know, they are the smartest animals after humans.

Click!

Squeak!

Who's brainy?

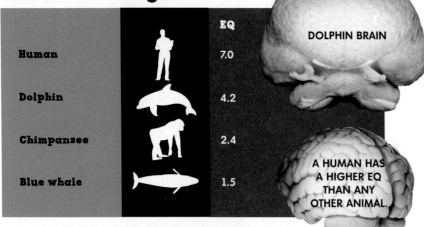

		EQ
Human		7.0
Dolphin		4.2
Chimpanzee		2.4
Blue whale		1.5

DOLPHIN BRAIN

A HUMAN HAS A HIGHER EQ THAN ANY OTHER ANIMAL.

EQ

Scientists have special ways to test intelligence in animals by comparing brain size and body weight. One measurement is called the EQ.

Half-asleep, but working!

A dolphin is a mammal. It must breathe air at the ocean's surface about every seven minutes. Only half its brain rests at a time, so it can continue to surface. Scientists recently saw dolphins swimming nonstop for five days straight! They were always using the parts of their brains that were awake.

sponge

Dolphins have figured out that holding sponges protects their noses!

Whistle!

Dolphins "talk" to one another using **different sounds**—whistles, clicks, and squeaks.

Scientists are studying dolphin noises, in the hope that we may one day be able to "speak dolphin."

It has been discovered that each dolphin has its own personal "NAME" call, used within its pod, or group.

Child's play
Dolphins recognize the differences between human adults and children. They are gentler with children.

Giant ocean

Until recently, not much was known about this huge fish

Marine biologist Dr. Tierney Thys has been monitoring and studying giant ocean sunfish since 2000. They look like enormous heads with fins! They are extremely successful, hold some impressive records, and grow to gigantic sizes—even though almost the only thing they eat is jellyfish!

1st Check out this record-breaking fish!

1 Sunfish are the heaviest bony fish on the planet.

2 Sunfish lay more eggs than any other vertebrate (animal with a backbone). One female may hold 300 million eggs inside her!

3 Sunfish multiply in weight from baby to adult more times than any other vertebrate.

From tiny, spiky baby to adult, a sunfish can grow to 60 million times its birth weight. That's like a human baby putting on the weight of six *Titanics*!

prove it!

Dr. Thys and her team have been studying the movements of giant ocean sunfish by tagging them. Through satellite tracking, they have found these giants living everywhere from the Arctic Circle to the tip of South Africa.

fish tags

Sometimes a scientist will cover a fish's eyes to make tagging less distressing for it!

sunfish

Sunfish are covered in irritating parasites. When the fish lie at the ocean's surface, seagulls pick the parasites off.

RESULTS One surprising discovery was that sunfish often lie motionless at the ocean's surface. People who saw them doing that had thought they were sick or dead! The tags showed that sunfish dive to 1,970 feet deep, and up again, to find food up to 40 times a day. They lie at the surface to warm up.

THIS MAY LOOK like a deadly stinging jellyfish.

IT IS ACTUALLY hundreds of zooids (tiny creatures)

that join together to form an even deadlier creature—

THE PORTUGUESE MAN-OF-WAR.

How old?

Some amazing clams have celebrated over 500 birthdays!

In 2006, scientists collected some ocean quahogs (a type of clam) off the coast of Iceland. They couldn't believe it when they discovered that one was 507 years old! They named it Ming.

The oldest human that ever lived died at age 122. That's old, right? Well, some ocean creatures can live to INCREDIBLE ages.

WOW! That's ancient! ➡

1 At 211 years old, a bowhead whale is the oldest recorded mammal on Earth.

2 One koi (a fish) named Hanako died at age 226.

They can tell us about life long ago.

prove it!

When you cut open a tree trunk, each ring shows a year of life. A clamshell also grows one ring each year. Dr. Paul Butler and his team at the School of Ocean Sciences at Bangor University in Wales counted and studied each clam ring under a microscope. What did they discover?

This is the real Ming!

The next time you have a bowl of clam chowder, you may be eating 500-year-old clams!

3 Black coral is the longest continuously living organism on the planet, at 4,265 years old.

4 Some species of sponge are thought to be 10,000 years old!

RESULTS

"One ring can give us information about pollution, climate change, and changing ocean currents for each individual year of a clam's life. Ming helped us go further back in time than ever before."

the

"A dive to the seafloor is like going into outer space—or even better, as there are so many beautiful and odd animals to discover in the deep sea. Even after a hundred dives, there's a sense of anticipation, of not knowing what you're going to see when the floodlights come on."

PROFESSOR CINDY LEE VAN DOVER

(see page 52 for more about Prof. Van Dover)

deep

Life in the

1,000 FT.
The deepest scuba dive ever was 1,082 feet (by Pascal Bernabé).

Few marine biologists have traveled to the deep ocean floor. At 200 feet down, the sea becomes black. The only light is made by deep-sea creatures, some of the strangest creatures on our planet.

5,000 FT.
Sperm whales dive to 8,200 feet.

Tallest mountain
Mount Everest is 29,035 feet high. If it sat on the seafloor, it would still be 6,500 feet under the surface.

10,000 FT.
The deep-sea anglerfish lives at 11,000 feet.

15,000 FT.
The dumbo octopus has been found at 13,000 feet.

How DEEP is the sea?

20,000 FT.

World's tallest building
Burj Khalifa, in Dubai, is 2,717 feet.

25,000 FT.
Deep-sea jellyfish live at 23,000 feet.

30,000 FT.

The deepest dive in a submersible was 35,787 feet (by James Cameron).

The Empire State Building is 1,250 feet.

35,000 FT.

When attacked, the atolla jellyfish sets off a display of bright lights that can

deep

Comb jellies

Scientists have seen these jellyfish produce flashing lights that run up and down their tentacles.

WHY DO THEY MAKE LIGHT?

1 Deep-sea animals use light to communicate with others of the same species.

2 Many fish also use light to lure prey toward them.

3 The hatchetfish uses its belly light for camouflage. The light hides its shadow from below.

Strange creatures

When the scientists in a deep-sea submersible turn on their vessel's lights, they sometimes see bizarre creatures lurking in the depths.

be seen 300 feet away. It attracts bigger predators, which eat its attacker!

Super**hot** vents

The deeper you go in the ocean, the colder it gets . . .

Vents like chimneys as tall as three-story houses stand in volcanic areas of the ocean floor. They belch out fluids at 660°F. Life couldn't possibly survive there, right? But scientists such as Professor Cindy Lee Van Dover have discovered a host of strange creatures living nearby.

Scientists used to think that all life needed the SUN to live. NOT ANYMORE!

prove it!

Prof. Van Dover regularly pilots the submersible *Alvin*. Her studies have shown that life can flourish on deep-sea vents, even without sunlight. Astronomers believe that Jupiter's moon Europa also has active vents. Does that mean there could be life there, too?

Lobsters covered in furry armor have been found!

Over 500 species have been found living on vents.

except by superhot vents!

RESULTS

How can there be life without sunlight? Prof. Van Dover and other scientists know how! They have found tiny bacteria that live on chemicals spat out by the vents. All the creatures that live there— shrimp, crabs, and snails as big as tennis balls—feed on the bacteria.

Giant clams 2 feet long have been spotted near vents.

11-foot-long tube worms live in warm water near vents, which are also called black smokers.

Let's dive!

The Alvin submersible carries two scientists and a pilot.

Sperm whales are massive—up to 66 feet long. Their heads take up nearly half of their whole bodies, and they can dive really, really deep.

Its brain is bigger than the brain of any other creature EVER found on Earth.

Heavyweight

An adult male sperm whale can weigh 50 tons. That's heavier than four African elephants! Its great weight is useful when it's diving.

50 TONS

Deep-sea diver

With a flick of its huge tail, a sperm whale can dive as deep as 8,200 feet. Humans struggle to reach depths of 160 feet without their ears popping! A sperm whale eats about a ton of food a day—mostly squid.

Sperm whale oil used to be used as soap, to light lamps, and—in both of the

A sperm whale's head **is** filled with **oil.**

When it's diving deep, the whale's lungs shrink to 1 percent of their normal size!

Scientists think that the oil may help whales handle the enormous water pressure at great depths.

The **clicking** sounds that a **whale** makes come from its oil.

Scientists have recorded the **clicks** of hundreds of sperm whales. They have realized that each **pod**, or family, has its own **language**. Whales click to show that they are in the same group.

The human breath-holding record is 22 minutes.

Hold it!

Sperm whales can hold their breath for well over an hour. Some scientists think that it may be closer to two hours! Whales spend 20 to 40 minutes at a time searching for food underwater.

HOW LONG ?

It appears that the deeper we explore, the weirder the

The Natural History Museum in London, UK, was given a rare hairy anglerfish specimen. The dead fish had such a big stomach that fish curator James Maclaine was extremely curious to know what it had swallowed!

When the anglerfish is hungry, it waves its glowing lure. Fish are attracted to the light, and the anglerfish gobbles them up whole!

Strange but true!

When a male anglerfish finds a mate, he attaches himself to her—and he never lets go! Once attached, he feeds off her blood. One female was found with seven males attached!

deep

James Maclaine took a CT scan of the anglerfish. He discovered that the 6-inch anglerfish had eaten a fish 10 inches long! The anglerfish's body had stretched to fit its gigantic meal. "There isn't a lot of food deep in the ocean, so when a fish comes along, the anglerfish tries to eat it—however big it is!" says Maclaine.

RESULTS

the anglerfish specimen

An anglerfish will try to eat anything it comes across. Some choke to death trying to force big fish down!

The CT scan showed that the anglerfish had eaten a fish called a softskin smooth-head.

WEiRd creatures

Check out these crazy creatures that lurk in the murky depths.

DARTH VADER?

Look familiar? This Vader look-alike jellyfish has 12 stomachs!

VAMPIRE

The mysterious vampire squid lurks in the dark depths. If threatened, it releases a glowing cloud of mucus to daze its attacker.

The weird but cute dumbo octopus hovers over the ocean floor, searching for prey. It is about the size of a beach ball.

Killer rabbit!

The rabbitfish is no cuddly pet. It has a venomous dorsal fin on its back.

of the deep

The sea pig has stubby little "legs" like a land pig's!

a tiny wood louse

This polychaete (a type of worm) looks like an alien from a movie! This ferocious predator has jaws that stick out. It lives on the muddy seafloor.

GIANT

The giant isopod is an enormous, 16-inch-long wood louse!

This fangtooth is the deepest-living fish ever found. When it closes its mouth, its teeth sink into deep pockets inside its head.

FANG TEETH

HELLO, HAIRY

The yeti crab was discovered living by superhot vents in the Pacific. Its hairy bristles are thought to filter poisonous water.

SEE-THROUGH

You can see right through this sea cucumber. When it swallows its food, you can watch it travel through its body!

NEED EXTRA TEETH?

The dragonfish LIVES 7,000 FEET BELOW THE SURFACE. It has **teeth** on its tongue!

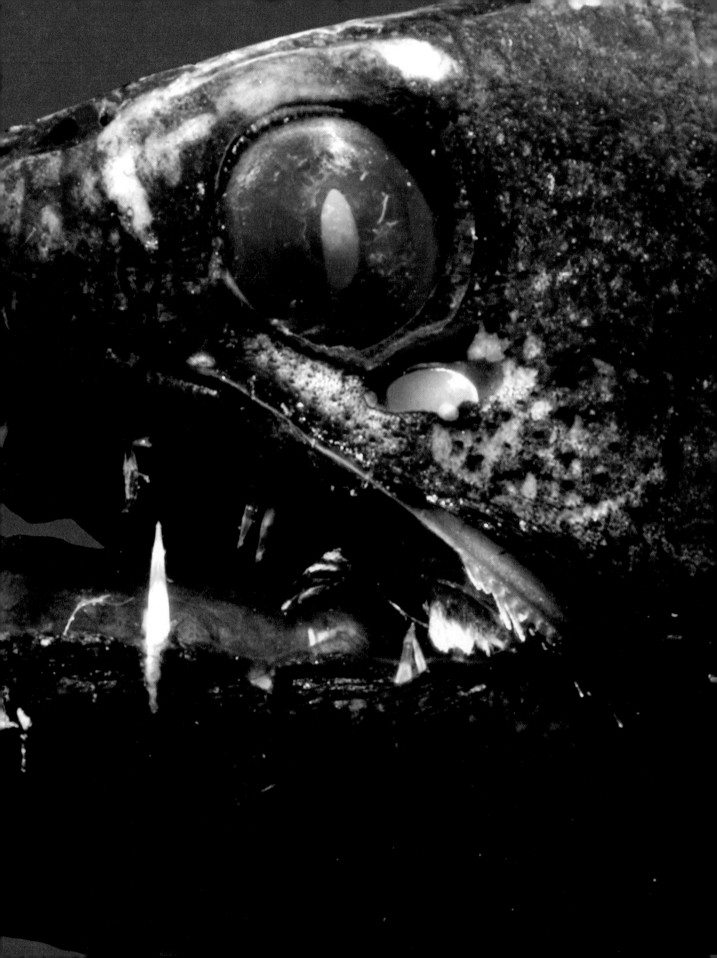

Glossary

antenna
A sticklike feeler on an animal's head that it uses to sense the world around it. The plural of *antenna* is *antennae*.

bacteria
Tiny living things that can be seen only with a microscope. Some can cause disease.

camouflage
Natural coloring that helps animals blend in with their surroundings.

climate change
Changes in Earth's weather patterns. These include rising global temperatures and changing patterns of rainfall.

coral reef
A strip of coral just below the surface of a body of water. Coral is a material made up of the skeletons of tiny sea creatures.

ecosystem
A community of plants and animals that live in a particular area and interact with one another and with their surroundings.

extinct
No longer in existence, having died out.

gauge
A way of measuring something.

habitat
The place or type of place where an animal usually lives and grows.

navigate
To steer along a particular path.

parasite
A living thing that lives and feeds on another living thing.

plankton
Tiny plants and animals that drift or float in oceans and lakes.

pod
A group of dolphins or whales that swim and feed together.

pollution
Harmful materials, like trash or chemicals, that dirty or poison the air, water, or earth.

polyp
A small sea animal with a round mouth surrounded by tentacles.

predator
An animal that hunts and eats other animals.

prey
An animal that is hunted and eaten by another animal.

satellite
A spacecraft that travels around Earth and collects scientific information or transmits messages.

school
A group of fish that swim and feed together.

species
A group into which living things of the same type are sorted.Members of the same species look alike and can mate with one another.

submersible
A vehicle that can travel deep underwater, often used for research and exploration.

swim bladder
The part of a fish's body that can be filled with air to keep the fish from sinking.

tagging
The act of attaching an identifying tag to an animal so that it can be tracked and studied.

tentacle
A long, flexible arm that is used to feel, hold, move, or sting. Octopuses and jellyfish have tentacles.

toxic
Poisonous to living things.

venom
Poison made by some animals, used to kill prey.

Index

Image credits

Alamy Images: 53 bl (AF archive), 56 cl, 56 r, 57 l (David Shale/Nature Picture Library), 36, 37 cl (Images & Stories), 17 (Jeff Rotman), 30 t bg, 31 t bg (Juniors Bildarchiv GmbH), cover main fish (Life on white), 38 t, 39 t (Mark Conlin), 6 bg, 7 l (Martin Strmiska), 4 bg, 5 bg (Michael Patrick O'Neill), 24 bg, 25 bg (Nuno Sa/Nature Picture Library), 3 b (Sami Sarkis Underwater), 51 br (Solvin Zankl/Nature Picture Library), 11 br inset (Tampa Bay Times/zumapress.com), 38 cr (Tosh Brown), 54 c, 55 c (WaterFrame); AP Images/Ifremer, A. Fifis: 58 br; Arthur Anker: 12 bg, 13 l; Brett Hobson: back cover Thys; Christian Sardet: back cover Sardet; Corbis Images: 53 br (Ralph White), 1 b, 44, 45 (Stephen Frink/sf@stephenfrink.com); Dr. Cindy Lee Van Dover: back cover Van Dover; Dr. Paul G. Butler: back cover Butler; Fotolia: 10 cr, 11 bc fish (bluehand), 15 cl (davidevison), 29 cr sharks (Ian Scott), 50 bl (Piktoworld), 52 bl (Quanthem), 29 shoe icon (rashadashurov), 28 cr icon (thailerderden10), 52 moon (Tristan3D), 38 bc (Valeriy), 37 bc, 46 t, 47 t, 56 water drops, 57 water drops (wawritto); Getty Images: 14 bg, 15 bg (A. Martin UW Photography), 32, 33 (Jason Isley/Scubazoo); iStockphoto: 29 seal icon (4x6), 40 chimp icon (A-Digit), 54 tr (Aaltazar), 13 tr (akinshin), 40 dolphin icon (albertc111), 50 t bg, 51 t bg (AM_Ellusion), 52 alien icon (andymo), 58 r (Antagain), 28 ct icons (appleuzr), 29 human hand icon, 50 tl (AskinTulayOver), 28 tr pink (assalve), 10 br (bennyartist), 46 br bg, 47 bl bg (BobHemphill), 34 tr (bulentgultek), 58 c bg (danilovil), 34 c bg, 35 c bg (DeepAqua), 30 cl (demarfa), 12 br (DSGpro), 28 c bg, 29 cr bg (egal), 20 t bg, 21 t bg (Ellende), 31 tr fish (eye-blink), 7 r bg (filo), pointing finger throughout (Freshvectors), 29 tennis ball icon (funnybank), 34 tl (GeorgePeters), 39 cl (gerasidi), cover blr fish, 3 t (GlobalP), 9 fg (GoodOlga), 42 l ribbon (Graffizone), 47 ice border (Grafissimo), 37 bl sign (grimgram), 28 sign (hidesy), 29 torpedo icon (highhorse), 8 bg, 9 bg (IBorisoff), 29 tire (icefront), 10 tr, 31 br (ifish), 58 bl (ilbusca), 24 t (iLexx), 25 crt (irin717), 31 cr (Iudex), 55 oil drops (kone), 37 tr (Kreatiw), 41 l (Laszlo Szirtesi), 50 br (Leontura), 59 cl (LindaZ), 21 br (Inzyx), 25 crb (loops7), 25 bl, 34 br (Lunamarina), 52 smoke, 53 smoke (LuVo), 47 bl fg (manjil), 10 cl (marcatkins), cover blb fish (marrio31), 40 br (mattjeacock), 11 tentacle (mj0007), 30 br (MogensTrolle), 2, 3 bg (Nastco), 13 shattered glass (-nelis-), 39 cr (Nikontiger), 40 whale icon (oktaydegirmenci), 47 cl soup (olegtoka), 30 bl, 31 bl (Predrag Vuckovic), 28 tiger fur (prmustafa), 6 l, 8 fg (Rainer von Brandis), cover bg coral reef (richcarey), 21 cr (robin819), 40 person icon (Robert Churchill), 25 cl (Roberto A Sanchez), 11 moon (samxmeg), 54 bl (Saro17), 15 cr, 63 tc (scubaluna), 13 br (Serp77), 25 br (Sezeryadigar), back cover bl fish (ShaunWilkinson), 1 tr (singularone), 19 br (snake3d), 55 clock icon (SoberP), 50 b bg, 51 b bg (SpinyAnt), 4 tl, 5 br (sserg_dibrova), 28 b (swartz), 39 br (SteveMcsweeny), 14 ink spots, 15 ink spots (stockcam), cover
cr fish, 11 shark, 11 bl (strmko), 21 boxing gloves (tacojim), 18 bg, 19 l bg (Tarasovs), cover blt fish, 20 t fish (tunart), 35 tr (Urs Siedentop), 29 handbag icon (UTurnPix), 27 tr (VictorburnsiWathende), magnifying glass throughout (VladislavMakarov), 21 crt (WhitcombeRD), 7 cl, 34 r, 35 l (Whitepointer), 21 tr (windwardskies), 46 br fg (xochicalco), 31 tl blood (yukipon); Jairo Rivera: back cover Rivera Posada; Kevin Raskoff/Arctic Ocean Diversity: 58 tr; MBARI © 2004: 58 center; Mike Johnson Marine Natural History Photography: 42 t bg, 43 t bg; NASA/Jeff Schmaltz, MODIS Rapid Response Team at NASA GSFC: 27 crt; National Geographic Creative: 53 tr (Emory Kristof), 20 cl shark (Stephen St. John); NIWA/Rob Stewart: 59 tr; Philippe Cousteau, Jr.: back cover Cousteau Jr., 4 bl; Science Source: 27 bl (Alexis Rosenfeld), 20 tl, 46 c, 47 cl (Andrew J. Martinez), 52 volcanic vents, 53 volcanic vents (B. Murton/Southampton Oceanography Centre), 59 br, 59 tl (British Antarctic Survey), 52 br (Colin Marshall/FLPA), 49 fg, 58 cl, 59 cr, 61 (Danté Fenolio), 26 bg, 27 bg (Dr. D. P. Wilson), 25 bc, 26 bl (E.R. Degginger), 52 c bg, 53 c bg (Explorer), 10 bl (Franco Banfi), 19 tl (Georgette Douwma), 51 bl (Gregory G. Dimijian), 21 crb (Jeff Rotman), 10 tl (Nancy Sefton), 21 tc (Neil G. McDaniel), 13 cr (Steve Trewhella/FLPA), 47 cr (Wanamaker et al/Bangor University); Shutterstock, Inc.: 22, 23, 62, 63 bg (Amanda Nicholls), 38 cl (Beverly Speed), 38 br (camelia), 20 br fish (Chanwit Polpakdee), 48, 49 bg (Christopher Waters), 30 cr (Daleen Loest), 29 tr fin (Dandesign86), 14 l (Dieter Hawlan), 40 c, 41 c (eZeePics Studio), 64 (holbox), 18 bl fg (James A Dawson), 38 bl (Joe Quinn), back cover tl manta ray (Kristina Vackova), 28 cl, 29 main shark (Matt9122), 43 br (Micha Klootwijk), 20 bl fish (Nantawat Chotsuwan), 15 straight tentacles, 63 tcl, 63 tcr (pick), cover t sharks (R. Gino Santa Maria), cover bg underwater, back cover bg underwater (Rich Carey), 19 bl (Richard Whitcombe), 15 curled tentacles, 63 tl, 63 tr (Stasis Photo), 40 cr (vasabii), cover br fish (Wiratchai wansamngam); Courtesy of Tag A Giant: 7 cr, 7 c, 7 b, 42 br; The Brain Observatory/Dr. Jacopo Annese: 40 tr; The Trustees of The Natural History Museum, London: back cover Maclaine, 57 br; Thinkstock: 31 cl (AlexanderCher), 11 r coral (joebelanger), 10 bg, 11 bg (nahpan), 1 tl (sserg_dibrova), 27 crb (zak00).

Thank you

Thanks to: Slaney Begley, Mae Dorricott, Katrina C. Hallett BSc (Hons) MSc, Karen Hood, Samuel M. Pountney BSc (Hons) MSc, Jack Sears-Stewart, Miranda Smith, Melissa Vural, and Rosie Young.